AMS IT'S OK TO HAVE BIG, CRAZY

RAZY DREAMS IT'S OK TO HAVE

HAVE BIG, CRAZY DREAMS IT'S

MS IT'S OK TO HAVE BIG, CRAZY

RAZY DREAMS IT'S OK TO HAVE

HAVE BIG, CRAZY DREAMS IT'S

MS IT'S OK TO HAVE BIG, CRAZY

RAZY DREAMS IT'S OK TO HAVE

HAVE BIG, CRAZY DREAMS IT'S

MS IT'S OK TO HAVE BIG, CRAZY

RAZY DREAMS IT'S OK TO HAVE

HAVE BIG, CRAZY DREAMS IT'S

MS IT'S OK TO HAVE BIG, CRAZY

RAZY DREAMS IT'S OK TO HAVE

TO HAVE BIG, CRAZY DREAMS

S0-BMS-459

This journal belongs to

Jacob,

a big, crazy dreamer.

Created, published, and distributed by Knock Knock
6080 Center Drive
Los Angeles, CA 90045
knockknockstuff.com
Knock Knock is a registered trademark of
Knock Knock LLC

© 2019 Knock Knock LLC
All rights reserved
Printed in China

No part of this product may be used or reproduced in any manner
whatsoever without prior written permission from the publisher,
except in the case of brief quotations embodied in critical articles
and reviews. For information, address Knock Knock.

Where specific company, product, and brand names are cited,
copyright and trademarks associated with these names are
property of their respective owners. Every reasonable attempt has
been made to identify owners of copyright. Errors or omissions
will be corrected in subsequent editions.

ISBN: 978-168349190-3
UPC: 825703-50192-6

10 9 8 7 6 5 4 3 2 1

IT'S OK TO HAVE BIG, CRAZY DREAMS

KNOCK KNOCK®
LOS ANGELES, CALIFORNIA

By 2022 - Do a reevaluation of office leasing
- Keep working hard - make that your
- Keep ~~~~ reputation
- keep in contact w/ the people who got
you here in the beginning
  - Cheryl Osborn
  - JC Carrion
- Don't worry about the outcome
- ONLY worry about what you CAN control
- Make fitness, work, family, friends your
- DUTY

The things that make us different, those are our superpowers—every day when you walk out the door and put on your imaginary cape and go out there and conquer the world because the world would not be as beautiful as it is if we weren't in it.

Lena Waithe

Stay afraid, but do it anyway. What's important is
Just do it and eventually, the

the action. You don't have to wait to be confident.
confidence will follow.   Carrie Fisher

Today's Note-to-Self: It's OK to wish that...

Our truest life is when we are in dreams awake.

Henry David Thoreau

Today's Note-to-Self: It's OK if people think I'm…

The world has told you lies about

how small you are. Heather Havrilesky

The universe is alive within us.... We are not figuratively, but literally stardust.

Neil deGrasse Tyson

Today's Note-to-Self: It's OK to do things like…

I will not take
"but" for
an answer.

Langston Hughes

Today's Note-to-Self: It's OK to be super excited about…

You're strong, you're a Kelly Clarkson

song, you got this.   Jonathan Van Ness

Today's Note-to-Self: It's OK to speak up about…

Your days are numbered. Use them to throw open the windows of your soul to the sun.

Marcus Aurelius

Don't let people talk you into doing the safe thing. Listen to what's inside of you and decide what it is that you care about so much that you're willing to risk it all.

Barack Obama

Today's Note-to-Self: It's OK that my bestie and I…

Today's Note-to-Self: It's OK to treat myself to…

The only courage you ever need is the
But if you don't have a dream

courage to fulfill the dreams of your own life.
today, start dreaming.   Oprah Winfrey

You must put your head into the lion's mouth if the performance is to be a success.

Winston Churchill

Today's Note-to-Self: It's OK if I start…

Today's Note-to-Self: It's OK to lose…

What and how
much had I lost
by trying to do
only what was
expected of me
instead of what
I myself had
wished to do?

Ralph Ellison

Today's Note-to-Self: It's OK to be hurt when…

I saw that my life was a vast glowing empty page

and I could do anything I wanted. Jack Kerouac

Today's Note-to-Self: It's OK to be, like,…

Living out loud is living a life that's bigger than yourself. Living out loud is living long after you're gone ... you leave something on this Earth that's bigger than yourself.

Viola Davis

Life is just a
big extended
improvisation.
Embrace the ever
changing, ever
evolving world
with the best rule
I've ever found.
Say "YES AND."

Jane Lynch

Today's Note-to-Self: It's OK to go all out and...

I got my first guitar when I was nine
Beatle, even though they had

because I wanted to be the fifth
already broken up.   Tig Notaro

If people say your dreams are crazy, if people laugh at what you think you can do, good. Stay that way. Because what nonbelievers fail to understand is that calling a dream crazy is not an insult. It's a compliment.

Colin Kaepernick

Today's Note-to-Self: It's OK that I'm so...

Do not confuse dreams with wishes.
visualize yourself being successful at
And dreams build

There is a difference. Dreams are where you
what's important to you to accomplish.
convictions.   Dolly Parton

Once I had asked
God for one or
two extra inches
in height, but
instead he made
me as tall as
the sky, so high
that I could not
measure myself.

Malala Yousafzai

Today's Note-to-Self: It's OK to believe…

Today's Note-to-Self: It's OK for me and you-know-who to…

I feel driven to express my strong opinions
when it's scary or inconvenient.
of which there were always many

and to challenge people's thinking, even
To remain stolid in the face of trolls,
but now even more. Aparna Nancherla

Today's Note-to-Self: It's OK if it takes me…

I am going to own my experiences. I'm going to pay attention to the reality of my life and the audacity of my dreams instead of the expectation I was raised with. I'm going to make space for the good and the bad of it, even the yucky scary fear-inducing parts, and embrace all the bits and all the questions.

Tracee Ellis Ross

Today's Note-to-Self: It's OK to feel all the feels when…

Take your risks now. As you grow older, you become more fearful and less flexible. And I mean that literally. I hurt my knee on the treadmill this week and it wasn't even on.

Amy Poehler

Today's Note-to-Self: It's OK to vent by…

I want to show that people need not
as long as they are not disabled

be limited by physical handicaps
in spirit.   Stephen Hawking

Make the most
of yourself by
fanning the tiny,
inner sparks
of possibility
into flames of
achievement.

Golda Meir

Today's Note-to-Self: It's OK to secretly hope…

Today's Note-to-Self: It's OK that I don't always…

You must do the thing you think

you cannot do. Eleanor Roosevelt

Today's Note-to-Self: It's OK to want...

You will never hear more people tell you that you're wrong than when you're succeeding.

Grimes

If your heart is in your dream

No request is too extreme

When you wish upon a star

As dreamers do

Leigh Harline and Ned Washington

Today's Note-to-Self: It's OK when...

It really is a test
of: How bad
you wanna do
this? I had to
remind myself
every day that I
didn't want to do
anything else and
that I was good
enough to do it.

Issa Rae

Today's Note-to-Self: It's OK to be confused about…

If one is lucky, a solitary fantasy can totally transform one million realities.

Maya Angelou

Today's Note-to-Self: It's OK to be seriously…

Love what you do and do what
who tells you not to do it. You
Imagination should be the

you love. Don't listen to anyone else
do what you want, what you love.
center of your life. Ray Bradbury

Today's Note-to-Self: It's OK to LOL about...

You could certainly say that I've never underestimated myself. There's nothing wrong with being ambitious.

Angela Merkel

Thankfully, dreams can change. If we'd all stuck with our first dream, the world would be overrun with cowboys and princesses.

Stephen Colbert

Today's Note-to-Self: It's OK that it drives me bonkers when…

Dumbo didn't need the feather;

the magic was in him.   Stephen King

Today's Note-to-Self: It's OK to wonder…

If you can't fly, run, if you can't run, walk, if you can't walk, crawl. But by all means, keep moving.

Dr. Martin Luther King, Jr.

It's up to you to make your life. Take what you have and stack it up like a tower of teetering blocks. Build your dream around that.

Cheryl Strayed

Today's Note-to-Self: It's OK if I stop…

If your dreams
do not scare you,
they are not
big enough.

Ellen Johnson Sirleaf

Today's Note-to-Self: It's OK that I didn't...

I know how it looks.
But just start. Nothing
is insurmountable.

Lin-Manuel Miranda

Oh, it's delightful to have ambitions. I'm so
be any end to them—that's the best of it.
you see another one glittering higher up still.

glad I have such a lot. And there never seems to
Just as soon as you attain to one ambition
It does make life so interesting.   L. M. Montgomery

Today's Note-to-Self: It's OK to think it's cool when...

You can't be
that kid standing
at the top of
the waterslide,
overthinking it.
You have to go
down the chute.

Tina Fey

Anything's possible, almost.

Marilyn Monroe

Today's Note-to-Self: It's OK because…

Today's Note-to-Self: It's OK to spend...

Hold onto your old friends. Kiss your mama.

Admit what your dreams are. Maya Rudolph

I've pushed my
comfort zone and
made it bigger
and bigger until
these objectives
that seemed
totally crazy
eventually fell
within the realm
of the possible.

Alex Honnold

Today's Note-to-Self: It's OK to have a…

Today's Note-to-Self: It's OK to wanna cry about...

If you take daring steps and are
have it all. But you might have

smart about it, you can probably
to wait a while.   Gail Sheehy

Today's Note-to-Self: It's OK to wear…

We must do extraordinary things. We have to. It would be absurd not to.

Dave Eggers

Today's Note-to-Self: It's OK that I kind of blew it when…

You are already
naked. There is
no reason not to
follow your heart.

Steve Jobs

Everything you can imagine is real.

Pablo Picasso

Today's Note-to-Self: It's OK blah blah blah…

Today's Note-to-Self: It's OK to rant about…

Whether you succeed or not is
Making your unknown known
keeping the unknown always

irrelevant—there is no such thing.
is the important thing—and
beyond you.   Georgia O'Keeffe

Today's Note-to-Self: It's OK if people don't…

No matter where
you are from,
your dreams
are valid.

Lupita Nyong'o

I believe I'm here for a reason. And I think a little bit of the reason is to throw little torches out to the next step to lead people through the dark.

Whoopi Goldberg

Today's Note-to-Self: It's OK to love…

At the age of six I wanted to be a cook.
And my ambition has been growing

At seven I wanted to be Napoleon.
steadily ever since.   Salvador Dalí

Today's Note-to-Self: It's OK to say screw it and…

I always did something I was a little not ready to do. I think that's how you grow. When there's that moment of "Wow, I'm not really sure I can do this," and you push through those moments, that's when you have a breakthrough.

Marissa Mayer

Today's Note-to-Self: It's OK to need less…

Remember
that great
expectations
create great
capabilities. If
you limit your
goals to what
you know you
can achieve, you
are setting the
bar way too low.

Ray Dalio

Today's Note-to-Self: It's OK that I haven't got…

I started writing a script at night and on
own short on a Christmas vacation. It was
and not good, but I did it and then

weekends, and eventually I shot my
imperfect and crazy and nerve-racking
just kept going. Ava DuVernay

To drive free! to love free! to dash
reckless and dangerous!

To court destruction with taunts—
with invitations!

To ascend—to leap to the heavens of
the love indicated to me!

To rise thither with my inebriate Soul!

Walt Whitman

Today's Note-to-Self: It's OK that I still…

It's better to go after something special and risk starving to death than to surrender. If you give up on your dreams, what's left?

Jim Carrey

Today's Note-to-Self: It's OK to freak out because…

Today's Note-to-Self: It's OK even if…

Dreaming, after all, is a form of planning.

Gloria Steinem

Today's Note-to-Self: It's OK to ask for…

So many of our
dreams at first
seem impossible,
then they seem
improbable,
then, when
we summon
the will, they
soon become
inevitable.

Christopher Reeve

The best you'll ever do is to understand yourself, know what it is that you want, and not let the cattle stand in your way.

Janet Fitch

Today's Note-to-Self: It's OK to hold on to…

Today's Note-to-Self: It's OK that I couldn't even...

Dreams express what your soul

is telling you. Eleni Gabre-Madhin

Today's Note-to-Self: It's OK when I miss…

I imagined
everything. I
never thought it
would happen.

Keith Richards

Today's Note-to-Self: It's OK to create…

It's never too late to have a happy childhood.

Tom Robbins

You have to
leave the city
of your comfort
and go into the
wilderness of
your intuition.
You can't get
there by bus,
only by hard
work and risk
and by not quite
knowing what
you're doing,
but what you'll
discover will be
wonderful. What
you'll discover
will be yourself.

Alan Alda

Today's Note-to-Self: It's OK to be pissed about…

At first people refuse to believe that a
begin to hope it can be done, then they
the world wonders why it was not

strange new thing can be done, then they
see it can be done—then it is done and all
done centuries ago. Frances Hodgson Burnett

I'm the kind of person who would rather get my hopes up really high and watch them get dashed to pieces than wisely keep my expectations at bay and hope they are exceeded.

Mindy Kaling

Today's Note-to-Self: It's OK to like it when…

Today's Note-to-Self: It's OK to think that…

So many
institutions in
our society need
reinventing.
The time has
come for a new
dream. That's
what being a
revolutionary is.

Grace Lee Boggs

Today's Note-to-Self: It's OK to give myself a break because...

The world has always been full of
OK, this is a democracy. But if
this is the time to

sheep. You want to be a sheep,
you want to find your own way,
do it.   Jane Campion

You are enough
just as you are.

Meghan Markle

Today's Note-to-Self: It's OK to spend too much time…

Today's Note-to-Self: It's OK to get mad when…

If you have a goal that is very, very far
you start to get there faster. Your mind

out, and you approach it in little steps,
opens up to the possibilities.   Mae Jemison

Today's Note-to-Self: It's OK to let go of...

Who said that ev'ry wish
Would be heard and answered
When wished on the morning star?
Somebody thought of that
And someone believed it
Look what it's done so far.

Paul Williams and Kenneth Ascher

The dream is
the truth.

Zora Neale Hurston

Today's Note-to-Self: It's OK that I…

Go forth and dream,
you big, crazy dreamer.